608

MY FIRST REFERENCE LIBRARY

INVENTIONS

by Julie Brown and Robert Brown
Adapted from Michael Holt's
Inventions

BELITHA PRESS

First published in Great Britain in 1990 by
Belitha Press Limited
31 Newington Green, London N16 9PU
Copyright © Belitha Press Limited and
Gareth Stevens, Inc. 1990
Illustrations/photographs copyright © in this
format by Belitha Press Limited and Gareth
Stevens, Inc. 1990
ISBN 1 85561 041 8
Typeset by Chambers Wallace, London
Reprinted in 1991 in Hong Kong
for Imago Publishing

British Library Cataloguing in Publication Data
CIP data for this book is available from the British
Library

Acknowledgements

Photographic credits:

Aspect Picture Library 5, 20, 55 right
Bridgeman Art Library 8, 21 bottom, 49
Elizabeth Whiting Associates 5
Mary Evans Picture Library 6, 37, 38, 41, 43
Tim Furniss 55 bottom
Susan Griggs/Dimitri Ilic 51
Robert Harding Picture Library 44, 58
Michael Holford 15, 17 top, 21 top, 22, 25, 33
Hulton Picture Company 51
Hutchison Library 17 bottom
Mansell Collection 53 bottom
NASA 56 right, 59
Planet Earth 48
Ronan Picture Library 7, 9 bottom, 53 top, 56 left
Science Museum Library 28
Science Photo Library 9 top
Spectrum Colour Library 35, 50
Topham Picture Library

Illustrated by: Peter Gregory, Pat Fogarty, Eugene
Fleury and Cathy Barrett

Series editors: Neil Champion and Mark Sachner
Educational consultant: Carolyn Kain
Editors: Kate Scarborough and Rita Reitci
Designed by: Groom and Pickerill
Picture research: Ann Usborne

Contents

Words found in **bold** are explained
in the glossary on pages 60 and 61

Inventions in Society

CHAPTER ONE

WHAT ARE INVENTIONS?

Stone tools, such as axes and knives, have been found with the bones of people who lived nearly two million years ago. These were among the first inventions. From the earliest times, people have made things that help them in their lives. People invent because there is a need for something new. Inventions can be for everyday use, for use from time to time, or just for fun.

▼ These people are using a lever to lift heavy blocks. A small force put on one end of the lever lets you move much heavier weights than you can by muscle power alone. You can pry open cans with levers. A see-saw is a lever that makes it easy to lift up your friend.

Invention or discovery?

Invention is not the same thing as discovery. Discoverers find things that we did not know of before. Inventors make use of known things in new ways. An invention is often made because of a discovery. Electricity was discovered, but the electric cooker was invented. How many inventions can you see? Homes have central heating and tele-visions. Offices and schools have computers and other machines. These are all inventions.

▲ Modern kitchens like this one have many useful inventions. They have gas or electric cookers, fans, ovens, telephones, electric lights, and other handy items.

▼ The computer – an invention with many uses.

Inventors

▶ On 14 December 1903, at
Kitty Hawk, North
Carolina, USA, the
Wright brothers made the
first powered flight in
their biplane, the Flyer.

Who invented what?

● Thomas Alva Edison, an
American, thought up
over 1,000 inventions,
such as the light bulb and
the gramophone.

● Walter Hunt invented
the safety pin one day in
1846 by simply twisting a
piece of wire.

● The escalator was
invented in 1900 by the
Waygood Otis Elevator
Company in America.

● Ernest Swinton
invented the tank in 1908,
first used by the British in
World War I.

How do inventors work?

Most inventors work alone, and
the invention is the idea of one
person. For example, Michael
Faraday invented the electric
motor in England. Sometimes,
two people invent the same thing
without knowing it. Inventors

may also work in teams. Many
inventors who shared their ideas
created the television.

Inventors must have an
understanding of science. They
use this knowledge to help them
invent. Alexander Graham Bell

◀ On 18 October 1892 Alexander Graham Bell first spoke into the telephone line connecting New York and Chicago.

Who invented what?

● An American, Hiram Maxim, invented the machine gun in 1883.

● Charles Gabriel Pravaz invented the hypodermic needle and syringe in 1853.

had to understand how electricity worked before he could invent the telephone.

▼ A hovercraft glides over water on a cushion of air that is blown down all around the craft. C. S. Cockerell invented it in 1953.

Patents and Sales

Fun and Games

● George Ferris invented the Ferris or Big Wheel in 1893.

● A man out of work invented Monopoly to make money.

Bicycle facts

● The safety bicycle with wheels of about equal size replaced the risky 'high-wheeler' in 1887.

● Bicycles first had air-filled tyres in 1888.

▶ The pennyfarthing bicycle, also called an 'ordinary', was developed in 1870. The front wheel was as tall as a man's shoulders.

Patenting an invention

Patents give inventors the right to make and sell their own inventions. They also keep other people from copying the inventor's ideas. To get a patent, inventors must prove their idea is original.

Selling an invention

It can be easy to patent an invention, but often hard to sell it. For example, in 1845, R. W. Thomson patented the idea of air-filled rubber tyres. But it wasn't until 1888 that air-filled bicycle tyres were sold by John Dunlop. In 1894, Guglielmo Marconi invented a way of communicating

▲ Velcro was invented by Georges de Mestral from Switzerland. He got the idea from nature. Two pieces of velcro stick together the same way burrs stick to animal fur – with many tiny hooks.

◄ Guglielmo Marconi (1874-1937), Italian inventor of the wireless, with one of his wireless sets on board a luxury yacht.

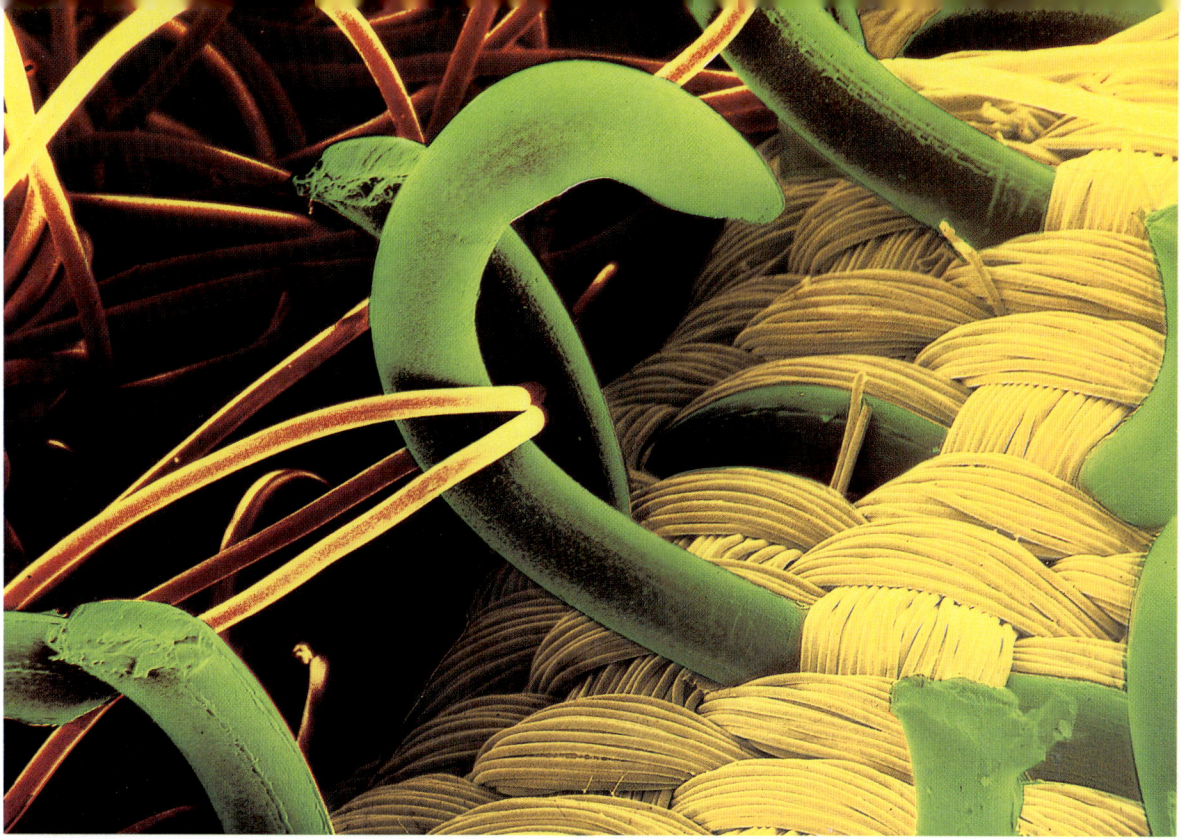

through **radio waves**. But the radio was not popular until the 1920s. If an inventor is lucky, many people will buy his or her invention. King Gillette, for instance, invented razor blades in 1895. By 1904, he was selling 12 million blades a year!

Making Tools and Trading

CHAPTER TWO

EARLY INVENTIONS

Early-toolmaking

About 10,000 years ago, people learned how to plant and grow crops. The first farm tools were simple sticks, used to dig the ground. Later, people made hoes and axes. They beat the iron out of **meteorites** and used the metal to make sharp blades. Hunters invented spears and the bow and arrow. People invented ways to make fire. They would hit two flint stones together to make a spark. Or they would rub sticks together until they glowed.

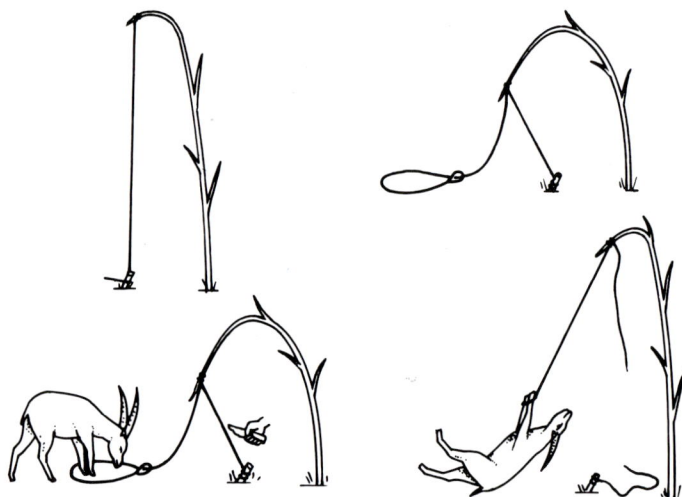

Cooking by Fire

When people invented ways to make fire, they soon discovered how to cook meat. They invented cooking pots for this, probably by coating straw baskets with clay.

The Spring Trap

▶ A small tree is tied down and a loop put on the end. The animal steps into the loop, the tie is cut and the loop jerks tight.

Barter and coins

Before people invented money, they traded, or bartered, to get what they wanted. If a person had meat and needed eggs, he would find someone else who had eggs and needed meat. In time, people began using **token** goods for trading, such as beads, pots or salt. These were easier to carry around. Later, people used gold and silver as money. The first coin, called the stater, was invented about 2,500 years ago in Asia Minor, known today as Turkey. The Chinese invented the first paper money over 1,000 years ago.

▲ Stone Age people using simple inventions to hunt game, start a fire, carry water, catch fish, and make a shelter.

▼ People once traded beads, teeth, and shells as tokens. Some Pacific islanders still use shells as tokens.

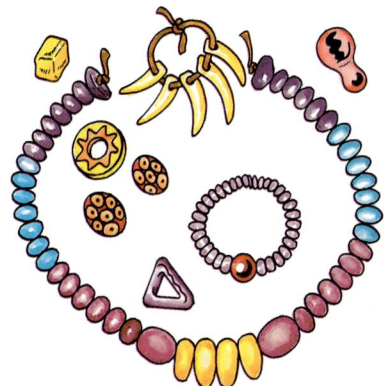

The Wheel

▼ Two oxen wearing a yoke can pull a wooden plough behind them, guided by the driver.

► North American Indians used horses to pull a loaded travois.

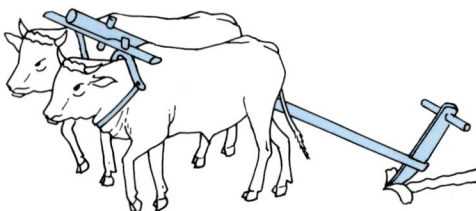

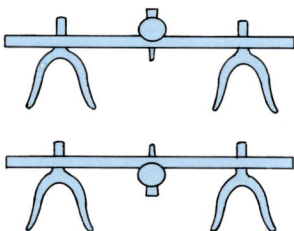

Long ago, people invented easier ways to carry large and heavy loads. Around 6,000 BC, they began putting **yokes** and **harnesses** on cattle to pull ploughs. Other people put pack saddles on horses so they could carry loads. Some Siberian and North American Indians still use the travois, a carrying sling dragged behind a horse. The sledge is another way of carrying loads over smooth ground such as snow and ice.

Using the wheel

People may have first used the wheeled cart in Mesopotamia (now Iraq) about 3,500 BC. These carts had an **axle** that turned with the wheels. The **Sumerians**

▲ In this Mesopotamian city, oxen pull a cart. The cart's fixed axle turns along with the wheels.

invented an axle that stayed still while only the wheels turned. This was the first great **mechanical** invention. The wheel was used in other ways too. People used water wheels to **irrigate** their crops and stone wheels to grind grain.

rotating axle

fixed axle

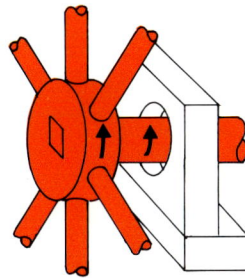

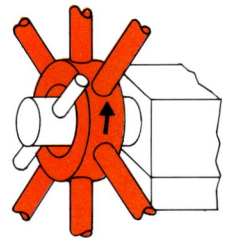

▲ This drawing shows the difference between the two kinds of axles.

◄ This early water wheel uses animal power to bring up the water.

Words and Numbers

▼ A simple puzzle shows how words can be made from pictures.

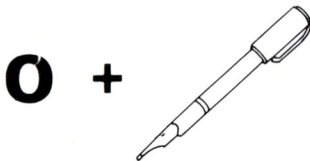

O + pen = open

P + ark = park

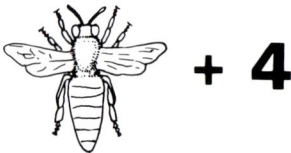

bee + 4 = before

▶ A diagram showing how our alphabet developed from earliest times.

Writing words and numbers
The Sumerians were the first to develop writing. They used picture symbols to stand for things, like a cow or a cart. For other words, they used a picture of something else that sounded the same. We use this same idea in some puzzles, where a picture of an eye can mean the word 'I'. The **Semites** invented an early alphabet that could write any word. Number systems were invented at about the same time as alphabets. The Sumerians, Chinese and other people all had number systems. The greatest number invention was **zero**. Using zero, people can write very large numbers.

Phoenician	Classical Greek	Etruscan	Classical Latin	Modern capitals
∢	A	A	A	A
ϑ	B	B	B	B
ϯ	Γ	⟨	C	C
⟃	E	ፆ	E	E
Ϥ	M	M	M	M
W	Σ	⟨	S	S

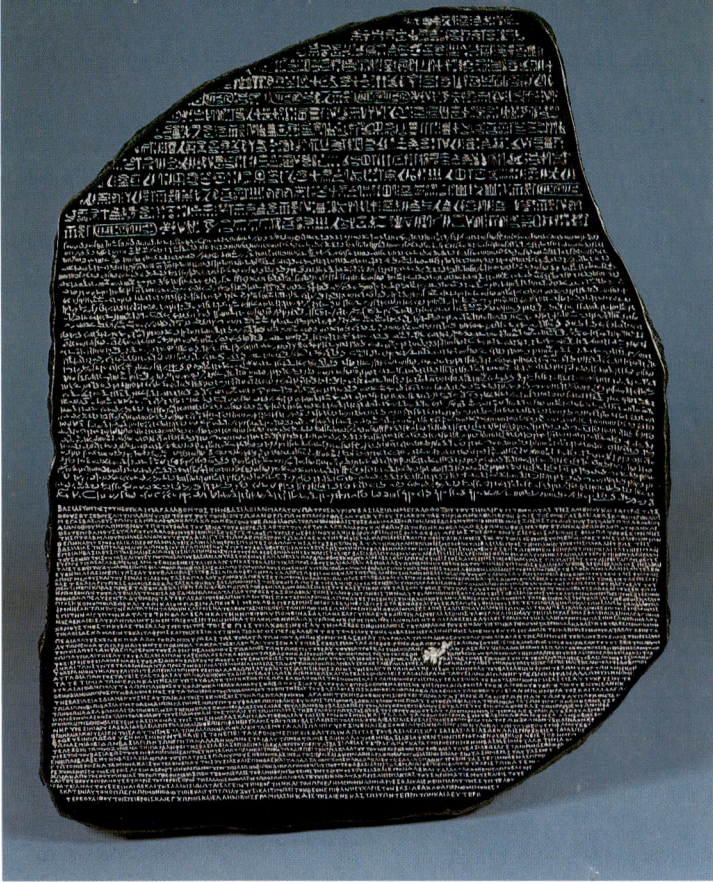

◄ The Rosetta Stone was discovered in 1799. It has the same message in three kinds of writing: Egyptian hieroglyphs (top), simple Egyptian writing (middle), and Greek (bottom). Someone who knew Greek then worked out the hieroglyphs.

Paper-making

Paper gets its name from papyrus, a reed the Egyptians used to make paper. The Chinese made paper from tree bark.

Paper facts

● The Moors introduced a paper-making process to Spain around 1150. By the 15th century paper mills had spread throughout Europe.

● Friedrich G. Keller, a German, invented a machine in 1840 to make paper from wood.

◄ Here is a Chinese adding machine called an abacus. It is similar to those used long ago. Each bead stands for a different number. The number arranged on this abacus is 1,532,786. The user flicks beads towards the centre to add up or take away.

15

City Builders

▶ The Archimedes Screw, invented around 250 BC by Archimedes. Turning the handle brings water up through the pipe and out at the top. It both irrigated and drained land in the Nile valley.

Both Greek and Roman city builders took the idea of the arch from the Egyptians. The Romans used the arch in a new way, for bridges. They put **vaulting** roofs, instead of beams, on their buildings. The Romans invented the crane for lifting heavy things. They also used a system of **pulleys**, called the block and tackle. The aqueduct, a stone canal used for carrying water, was also a Roman invention.

Greek inventions

Archimedes was the greatest inventor in ancient Greece. He invented a machine that lifts water out of rivers for irrigating the land. It is still used along the River Nile today. He was also the

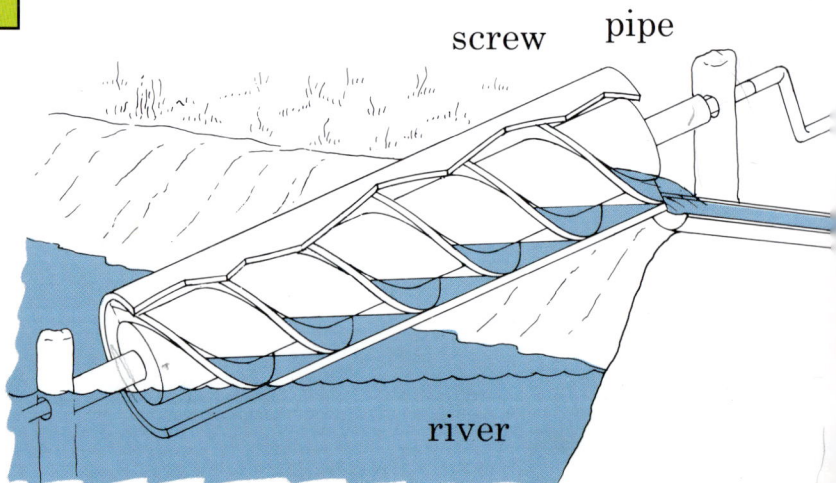

screw   pipe

river

first person to work out how levers and pulleys worked. The Greeks invented a better clock, first used by the Egyptians around 1500 BC. It uses dripping water to tell time and is called a *clepsydra*. The Greeks also invented the ruler and compass to help in accurate drawing.

▲ A Roman aqueduct built about 2,000 years ago, in France, to carry water.

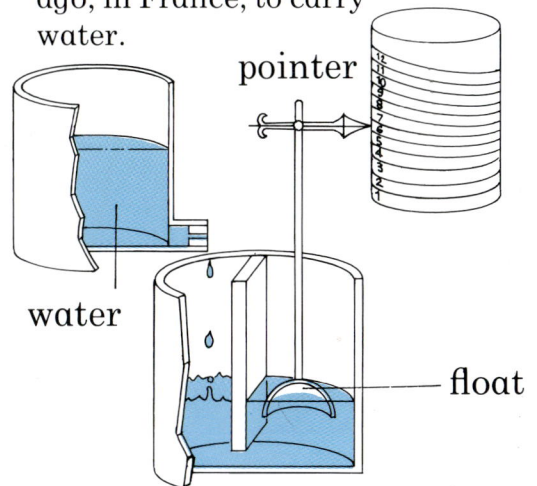

▲ A Greek *clepsydra,* or water clock. Dripping water lifted the pointer. The line it pointed to told the time.

◄ The *shaduf* is a bucket on a long pole. A weight on one end helps the man lift water from the river to irrigate his field.

17

Early Transport

CHAPTER THREE

INVENTION AND TRAVEL

Getting around on land

For thousands of years people have ridden horses. **Stirrups** were first added to saddles in India, which made riding horses easier and safer. The horse-collar, a sixth-century Chinese invention, made it possible for horses to pull ploughs and carts. Horseshoes, invented by the Romans, helped horses walk on the stone roads.

Getting around on water

Early towns were usually built on the banks of rivers, such as the Tigris, the Euphrates and the Nile. People learned to cross over

▼ A modern blacksmith nails a horseshoe onto a horse's hoof. The nails go into the hoof's hard horn rim. This does not harm the horse in any way.

▲ Sails helped the Nile boats go much farther.

◄ A map of Mesopotamia. The Sumerians lived here between 4,000 BC and 3,000 BC.

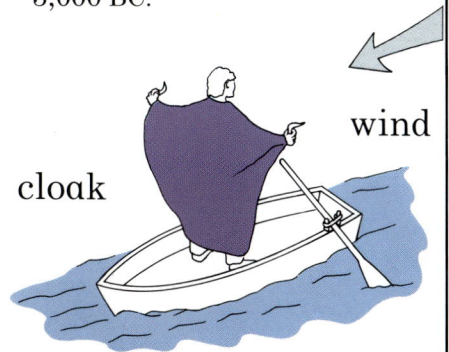

Map labels:
- Lake Urmia
- Tigris R.
- MESOPOTAMIA
- Euphrates R.
- Diyala
- MEDITERRANEAN SEA
- Orontes R.
- Babylon
- Jerusalem
- PERSIAN GULF

The Fertile Crescent
Earliest Agricultural Sites
Earliest Cities

0 100 200 300 400 500 kms
0 50 100 150 200 250 mls

wind

cloak

Inventing the sail

Probably someone wearing a cloak stood up in his boat. The wind caught his robes and blew the boat along.

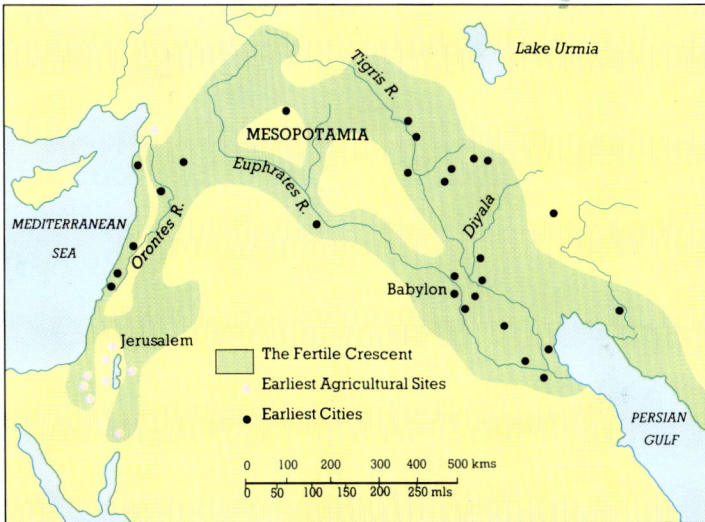

water by using logs as floats. The first boats were canoes dug out of logs. People made the first rafts from reeds, **bamboo**, or wood. The Egyptians built river boats out of reeds. For fishing from boats, early fishermen invented nets, rods, lines and hooks.

Sailing Ships

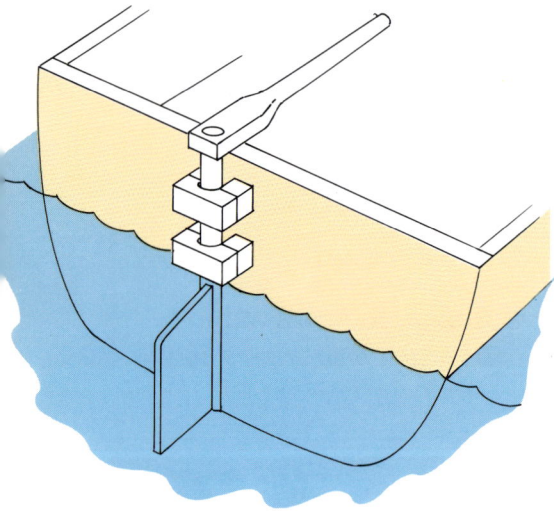

The first sailors were probably the **Cretans**. They sailed over the Mediterranean Sea in **galleys** powered by oars around 3,000 BC. By 1,500 BC, the Phoenicians had invented planks to make ships, called biremes, that had two levels of oars on each side. The Greeks developed a galley that moved by both oars and sails. It could travel great distances.

Improvements in sailing

By AD 800, the Vikings invented longboats with sturdy **keels**. A sailor steered the longboat by an oar attached to the starboard, or right-hand side. Around AD 1100, the Chinese invented the first true **stern-post** rudder. This made steering easier. Sailors invented ways of finding their

▲ When the handle of a rudder is pulled to the left, the rudder moves right. This steers the boat to the right.

▶ Arabs have been sailing *dhows* like this for over 1,000 years.

▲ This bowl shows a Greek galley with oars, sails and a battering ram.

◄ Viking longboats sailed across the Atlantic.

▼ An early map of the world from AD 40.

route by using the stars as a guide. Soon people made maps of the sea and the coasts, as well as maps of the stars. So began the science of **navigation**.

Finding the Way

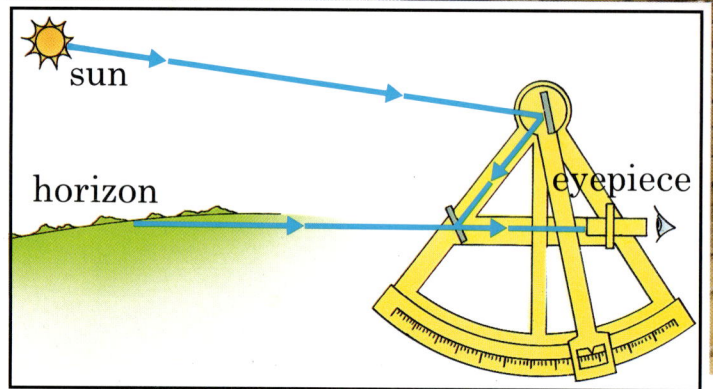

A sextant

This astrolabe was made in Germany in 1548 by George Hartman.

Several inventions helped sailors find their way at sea. The astrolabe, probably invented around 150 BC by the Greek Hipparchus, was used by sailors to help work out the position of their ship. The Chinese invented the compass. They found that a piece of **magnetic** iron, called a lodestone, when balanced on a needle, always points north. A compass card, invented in the 13th century, shows the directions north, south, east and west.

lodestone

needle

Using a Sextant

The sailor lines up the Sun with the horizon by moving a mirror and then reads the angle. This tells him the position of the ship.

◄ The magnetic lodestone turns on a needle point. You can read the direction on the compass card. ▼

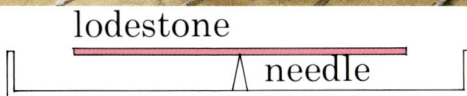

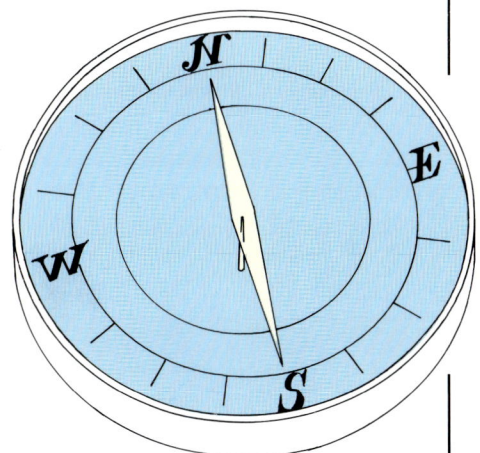

The compass made navigation easier and long voyages possible.

Later inventions

John Hadley in England and Thomas Godfrey in the United States invented the sextant. With it, sailors could use the Sun or stars to help them find the ship's exact location north or south. Staying on their route meant that ships with cargo could reach their ports without getting lost.

Compass

Slings and Catapults

CHAPTER FOUR

INVENTIONS FOR WAR

From early times, people have invented weapons for war. The sling, a simple invention, could be used to hurl stones farther and harder than by hand. About 3,000 BC, four-wheeled chariots carried soldiers into battle. By 1,100 BC, the Persians made lighter and faster chariots with two wheels and an axle that turned. Soon after people learned how to make bronze, they invented swords. Roman soldiers developed an early battering ram – it was a tree trunk tipped with metal that swung from ropes. They also built long ladders for climbing up enemy city walls.

▲ This Roman soldier wears iron bands on leather as armour and a bronze helmet.

The Crossbow

The crossbow was invented by the Chinese around 500 BC. It was more accurate and could shoot arrows farther than a normal bow.

Catapults

The Greeks used catapults that could fire stones or arrows. The Chinese designed the trebuchet, a giant slingshot that could throw things even farther. The Romans built a small catapult, called an onager, powered by twisted ropes.

▲ An early Persian war chariot from about 1,100 BC. It had only two wheels. One warrior would drive the chariot in battle. The four horses that pulled it could gallop at 40 mph!

◄ This catapult is being wound up, ready for firing. By twisting the ropes, the soldiers prepare the catapult to hurl large boulders towards their enemies.

25

Guns and Cannons

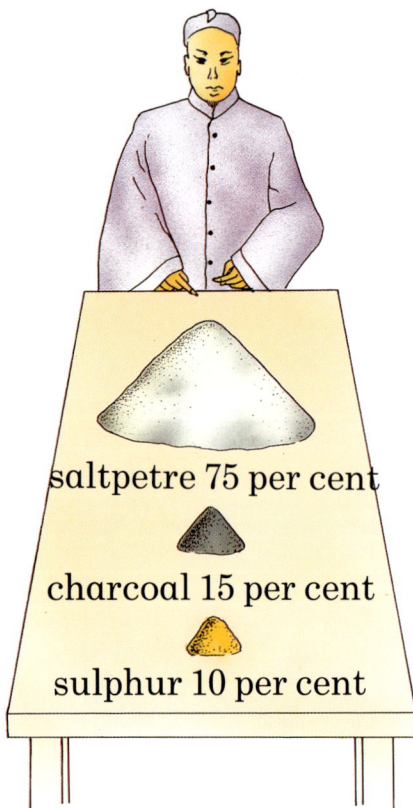

The Chinese invented gunpowder, the first man-made explosive, around the ninth century AD. They used it for fireworks and rockets. When gunpowder came to Europe in 1242, people used it to make weapons.

Cannons on land and sea

On land, cannons soon replaced the catapult and the battering ram. Cannons were easier to move around. Cannon balls could smash down the walls of castles and cities. At sea, cannons replaced the older fighting methods of ramming and setting other ships on fire. Ships with cannons could sink other ships at a distance. The first hand-held gun was the musket. It works like a cannon but fires smaller balls.

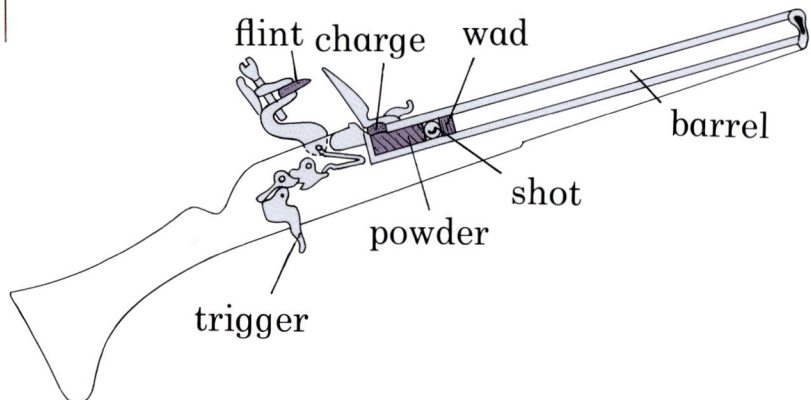

saltpetre 75 per cent

charcoal 15 per cent

sulphur 10 per cent

▲ The Chinese made gunpowder by mixing these ingredients. When lighted it explodes.

► A musket is really a small cannon.

flint charge wad

barrel

shot

powder

trigger

The big bang in science

Gunpowder brought many important changes to science. The making of gunpowder led to the science of chemistry. The need to fire cannon balls accurately led to the sciences of **ballistics** and of explosives. Scientists also learned about heat when they made cannons.

▲ During sea battles it was always best to have a wind to fill the sails. Most of the cannons fired from the sides of the ship.

▼ Gunners had to work out where each cannon ball would land. This led to the science of ballistics.

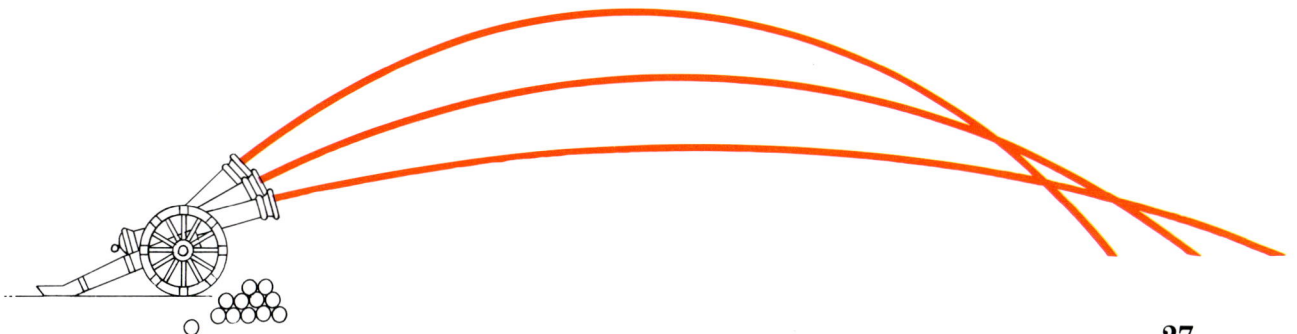

Leonardo da Vinci

CHAPTER FIVE

THE ADVANCE OF SCIENCE

Leonardo da Vinci (1452-1519) was an architect, a craftsman, an artist and an engineer. He was a great genius of the **Renaissance** period. He filled many notebooks with his ideas and sketches. Most of his inventions were way ahead of their time and were not built.

Leonardo's inventions

His great invention on paper was the flying machine. After watching the way birds flew, Leonardo made many models of flying machines. All of his plans were superbly drawn. They include:

Backward writing

Leonardo wrote most of his notes backwards with his left hand, and read them with a mirror.

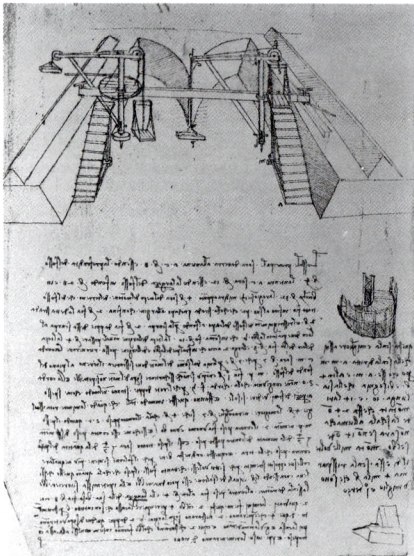

▲ A page from one of his notebooks showing sketches and backward writing.

● An armoured car driven by cranks and pedals
● An alarm clock that worked by tilting the sleeper's bed
● A diving suit that let a person stay underwater for four hours

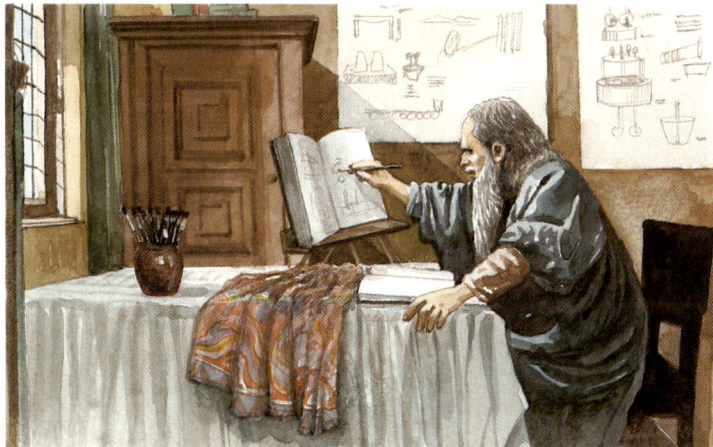

Leonardo worked for some of the most powerful princes of his day, such as Lorenzo the Magnificent and King Francis I of France.

- A submarine
- A crude kind of helicopter
- Pumps to empty water out of mines
- Rolling-mills to shape metal into sheets

▲ In 1988, a wooden model of a flying machine was built based on a design by Leonardo. It looks very much like a bird's wings but would not have flown.

◄ Leonardo was a great artist. He painted the *Mona Lisa,* one of the finest paintings in the world. He was also a great scientist and studied geology, biology and mathematics.

Lenses

The Egyptians invented glass before 3,000 BC. Later, the Arabs discovered how to grind glass into lenses. Lenses made small objects look larger. By 1350, many Italians wore eye-glasses, or spectacles.

Around 1600, a Dutch lens grinder's assistant saw that looking through two lenses made faraway things seem much nearer. In 1609, Galileo Galilei used the discovery to make his first telescope. He used it to study the stars and the planets.

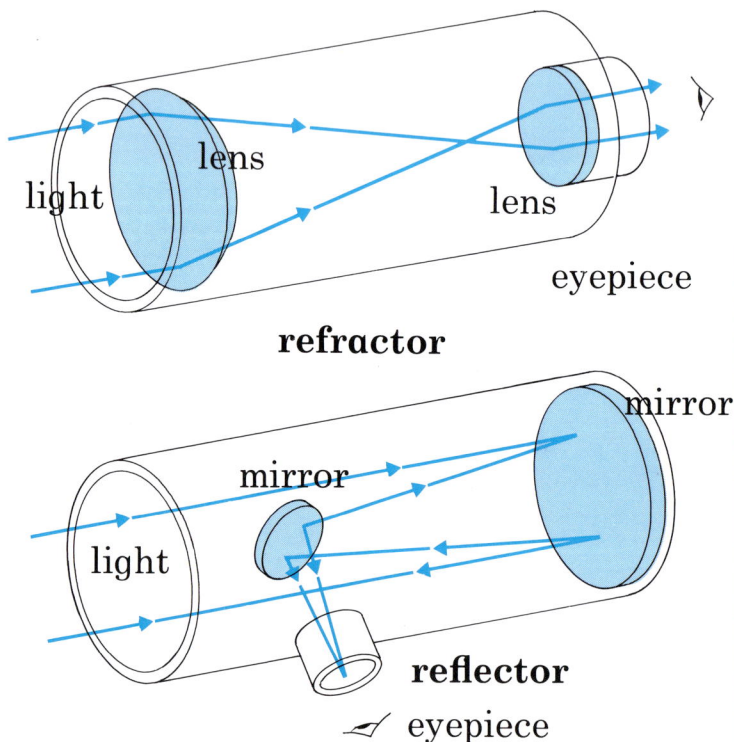

▲ This pair of simple spectacles was made in the early 1500s.

▶ The simple refracting telescope (upper) is called the Galilean, after the famous astronomer. The big lens magnifies the image. In the reflecting telescope (lower), a mirror magnifies the image.

refractor

light   lens   lens   eyepiece

reflector

light   mirror   mirror   eyepiece

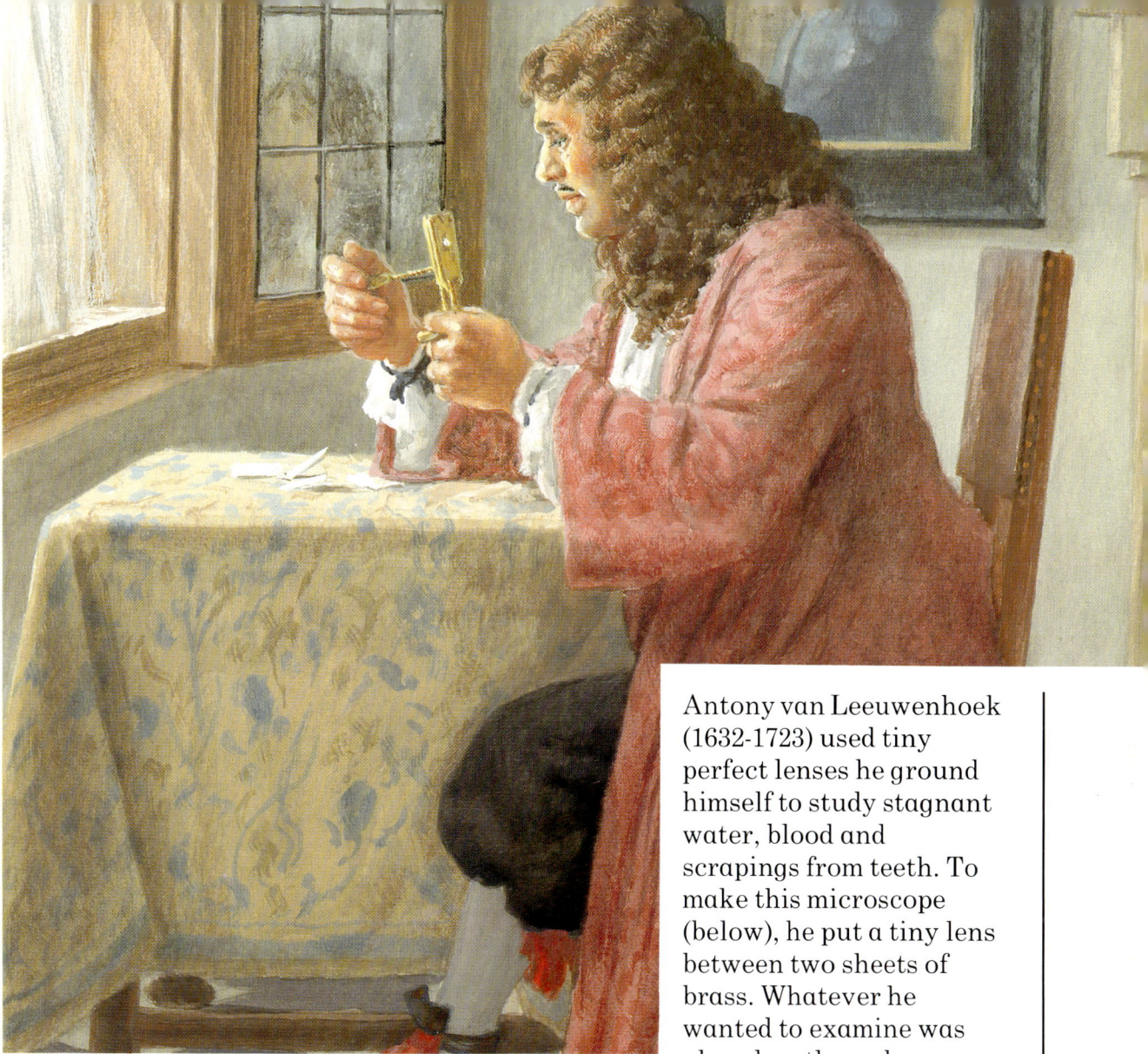

Antony van Leeuwenhoek (1632-1723) used tiny perfect lenses he ground himself to study stagnant water, blood and scrapings from teeth. To make this microscope (below), he put a tiny lens between two sheets of brass. Whatever he wanted to examine was placed on the rod.

The world of small things

The first microscope was probably made in 1590 by a Dutch spectacle-maker. Antony van Leeuwenhoek, also Dutch, made tiny lenses that **magnified** things over 200 times. He saw things that no one had seen before, like **bacteria** and tiny water fleas living in a drop of water!

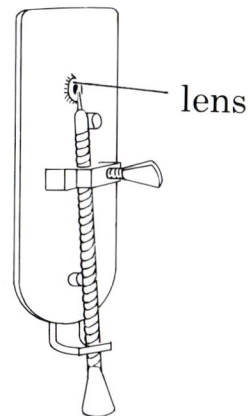

lens

Telling the Time

▼ Galileo swings a simple pendulum. In 1657 Christian Huygens designed the first pendulum clock.

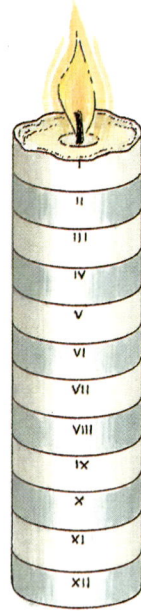

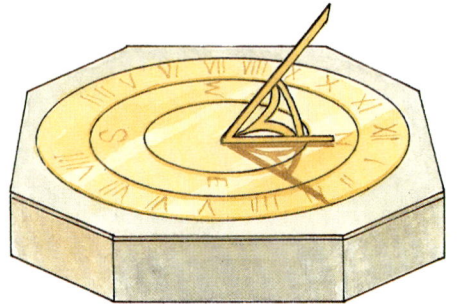

The very first clocks were sundials that told the time from shadows cast by the Sun. Next came candle clocks that burned down to hour marks, water clocks that dripped at a certain speed, and hour-glasses filled with sand. Later mechanical clocks were invented. These worked on a system of springs, wheels and **gears** that had to be wound up. Hands on the clock face moved around to show the time. Churches used these clocks. Galileo thought of using a hanging pendulum in clocks.

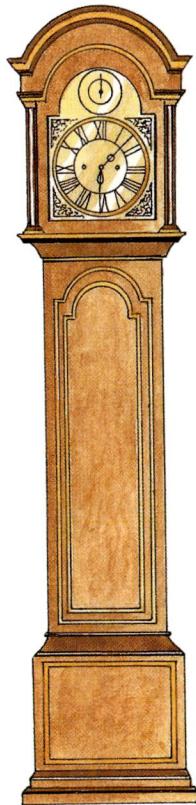

◀ Early and recent clocks: candle clock, sundial, hourglass, wristwatch, digital clock and pendulum clock.

▲ Salisbury Cathedral's clock, made in 1386, is the world's oldest working clock.

▼ This is the fourth chronometer that John Harrison designed. It was so accurate that it kept time to within one-tenth of a second per day!

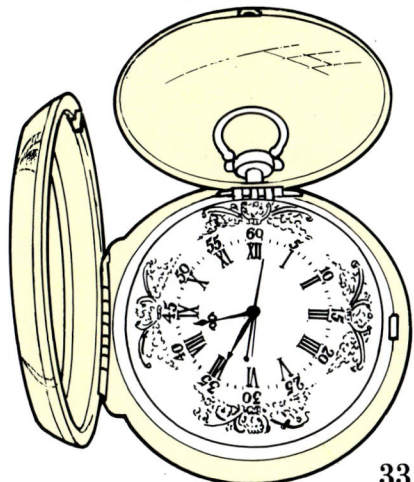

Timekeeping for navigators

Sextants were used to tell a ship's position north or south. But to work out its position east or west, navigators needed to know the exact time. Robert Hooke, of England, replaced the clock's pendulum with small wind-up gears. This clock was called a chronometer. The first truly accurate one was made by John Harrison in 1764. It was the size of a pocket watch and kept nearly perfect time. Navigators could use its exact time to work out their ship's position correctly.

33

Water and Wind

In the Middle Ages, water-mills were used as a source of power. Nearly every wealthy household had a water-mill and a miller to operate it. Mills used **trip hammers** and **cranks**, both invented by the Chinese. The water-mill was used for grinding grain and pounding metal. Men called millwrights travelled around the country making and repairing mills.

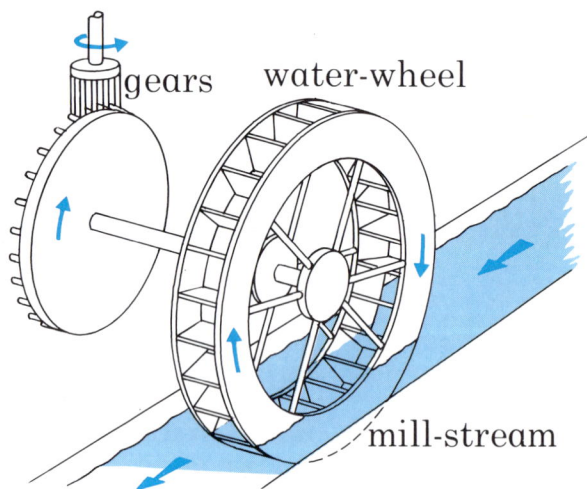

▶ The water wheel shown here is turned by water flowing under it. The wheel turns the gears.

▶ The typical medieval manor house had a water-wheel. It was used to power simple machines, like turning roasting spits in the house.

◄ Windmills, like this one in Holland, have four sails made of wooden slats that catch the wind. The mills once pumped water or ground grain.

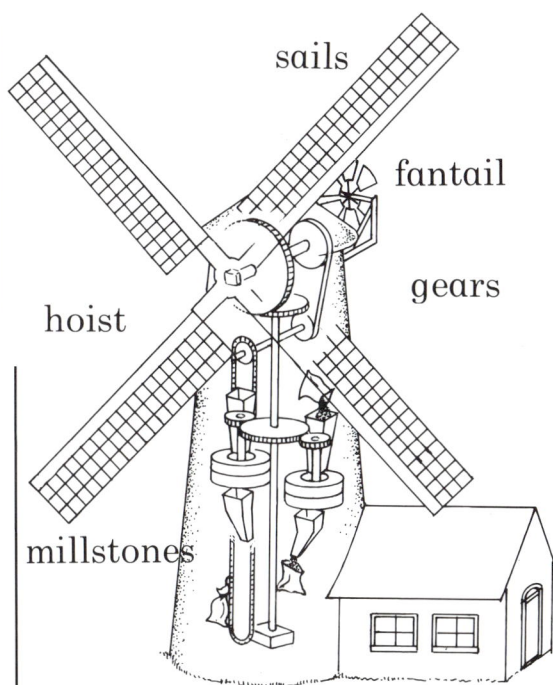

sails

fantail

gears

hoist

millstones

Windmills

Windmills, like sails, make use of the power of the wind. The Chinese used windmills for irrigating the land and for grinding grain. By 1150, windmills were used in England, France, Holland, Belgium and Spain. Like water-mills, they ground grain. Windmills were also used for washing clothes, blowing air into furnaces, and sawing wood. In the 18th century, windmill power was used to spin and weave cloth.

▲ This sketch shows how the windmill works. A fantail turns the top of the windmill so the sails always face into the wind. The sails turn the cogs and gears that give power to the millstones.

From Printing to Air Pressure

Early printing

The Chinese invented printing with wooden blocks about AD 770. Pi Sheng made movable letters from clay in 1040 for printing Buddhist prayers.

Printing

Around 1440, a German goldsmith, Johannes Gutenberg, invented a new way of printing. He made individual metal letters that could be arranged in any way in a frame. In this way, he could make up many different pages, using the metal letters again and again. He also invented the printing press. The first book he printed was the Bible.

Other inventions

Galileo invented the water **thermometer**. It had a bulb as big as a hen's egg and a long tube. Later, Gabriel Daniel Fahrenheit made the mercury thermometer and a temperature scale that we still use. One of Galileo's pupils invented the barometer to

▶ Here is Otto von Guericke's famous experiment. In the German emperor's park, he showed the effects of a vacuum. The air pressure holding the globe together was stronger than even 16 horses!

◄ Johannes Gutenberg shows two printed pages to his friends.

▲ Barometers like this one are used to predict the weather from changes in air pressure.

measure **air pressure**. Otto von Guericke of Germany invented an air pump to make a **vacuum**. In an experiment in 1654, he pumped all the air out of two half-globes of copper. The air pressure outside held the halves together so tightly that not even sixteen horses could pull them apart!

Coal-mining

wire gauze

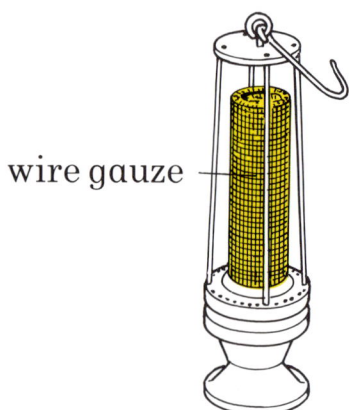

▲ Sir Humphry Davy's safety lamp. The wire screen kept the lamp's flame from causing gas explosions in mines.

▶ Long ago, men dug out coal using simple tools in mines like this. Today they use machines.

CHAPTER SIX

THE INDUSTRIAL REVOLUTION

The swift spread of machines and factories in the 1700s is called the Industrial Revolution. It gave work to the many country people who had moved to the cities of Europe and North America. The wooden machines that were being used soon wore out, so machines were made of iron, a stronger material. But iron had to be **smelted** with huge fires. The smelter fires burned coal that was dug out of the ground and hauled around by horse-drawn wagons. The coal-mines had to be kept dry

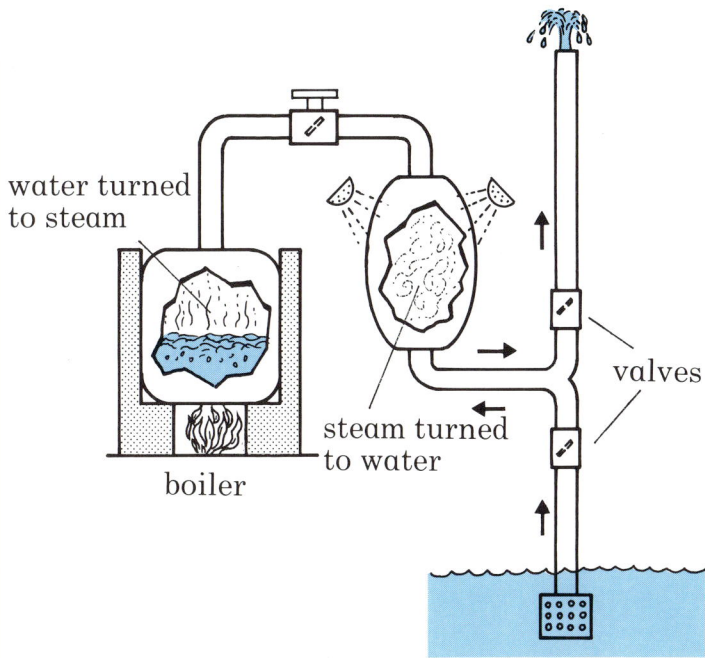

water turned
to steam

boiler

steam turned
to water

valves

◀ Savery's steam-engine pumping water out of a mine shaft. Steam turned to water in the tank, making a vacuum that sucked water up the pipe into the tank. Then more steam drove the water out of the tank and up the pipe. Valves controlled the flow of steam and water.

so the miners could work. But water kept leaking in.

Mining safety

In 1698 Captain Thomas Savery of London patented a steam-driven engine that pumped water out of the mines. He called it 'The Miner's Friend'. Thomas Newcomen designed a better pumping engine, but it burned a lot of coal. Later, James Watt invented a much better steam-engine. A big danger for miners was that the lamps they used set off gas explosions in the mines. Sir Humphry Davy invented the safety lamp in 1815.

▲ Newcomen's steam-engine pumping water out of a mine. Unlike Savery's engine, this one worked above the ground.

The Age of Steam

▶ James Watt's steam-engine used a separate condenser for cooling steam. This allowed the heated cylinder to stay hot, so the engine worked much better.

The steam-engine on land

James Watt, an instrument maker in Scotland, had an idea for improving the steam-engine. Instead of having the steam heat and cool in the same **cylinder**, he used a second cylinder where the steam could **condense** back into water. With this invention the modern steam-engine was born. Watt also invented the governor. This made the engine run at a steady speed. In 1801, Englishman Richard Trevithick first used a steam-powered carriage. George Stephenson invented the exhaust funnel so the fire burned hotter, giving the steam-engine more power.

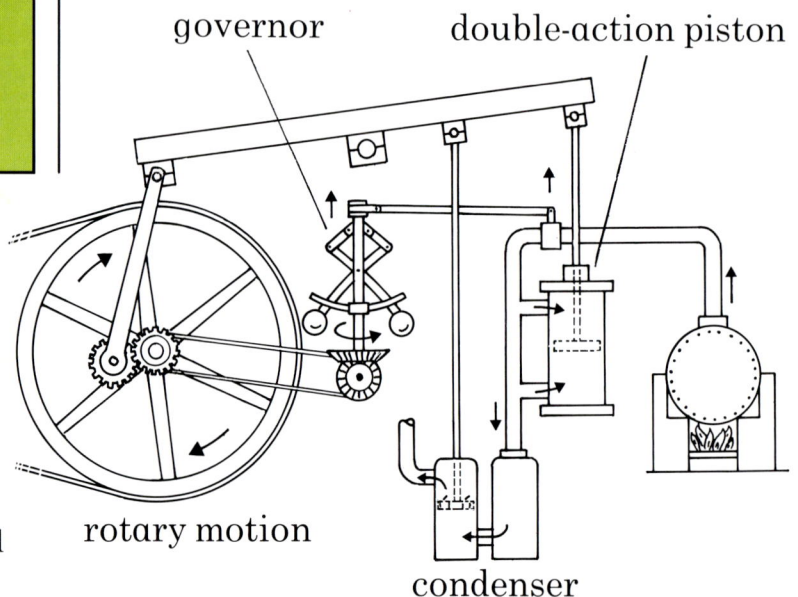

governor

double-action piston

rotary motion

condenser

GEO. STEPHENSON'S ROCKET. 1829.

Steamboats

Denis Papin invented a steam-powered boat with a paddle wheel in 1707, but angry boatmen wrecked it because they thought it would hurt their business. In 1807 Robert Fulton built the first steam-powered boat for paying passengers – the *Clermont*.

▲ The *Rocket* – a famous 'Puffing Billy'.

Sea-going facts

● John Fitch invented the passenger steamboat. It was not popular and he died penniless.

● The *Clermont* was the first paying-passenger steamboat.

● The first steamer to cross the Atlantic was the *Savannah*. It made the trip in 29 days.

◀ The *Clermont* – first passenger-carrying steamship.

Spinning

The textile revolution

The Industrial Revolution's biggest impact was on the industry that made cloth, or textiles. In the 1700s cotton, picked by slaves, was shipped from North America and the West Indies to England. There it was made into **fabric**. Early spinners and weavers worked in their own homes. Later, steam-powered machines moved cloth-making into textile factories.

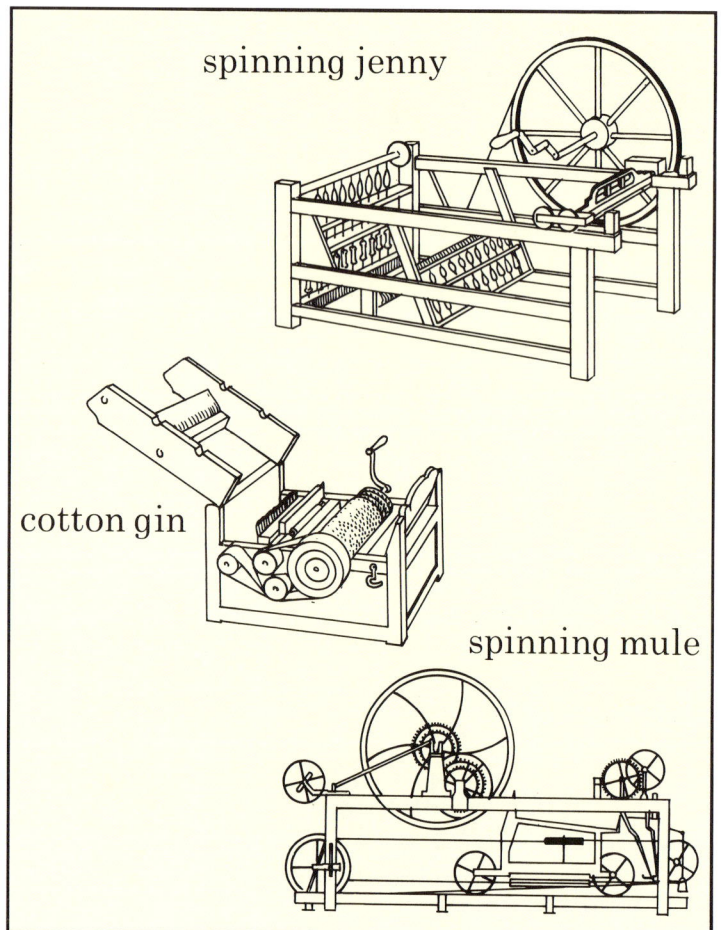

Textile facts

● The spinning jenny could spin 16 threads at one time, instead of only one like the old spinning wheels. 'Jenny' was a nickname for 'gin' or 'engine'.

● The spinning frame was patented in 1769. It used water power for spinning thread.

● Eli Whitney's cotton gin feeds cotton fibre through a row of saws. Teeth on the saws pull cotton from seeds.

● The spinning mule, invented in 1779, was a combination between the spinning jenny and the spinning frame. It made very fine yarn.

spinning jenny

cotton gin

spinning mule

Speeding up production

In 1767, the spinning jenny was invented to spin cotton threads swiftly into **yarn**. Other devices invented were the spinning mule and the spinning frame. In 1789, Edmund Cartwright invented the power loom. He used a steam-engine to power a weaving machine. In 1793 Samuel Slater built the first cotton mill and Eli Whitney invented the cotton gin. This mechanically removed the seeds from the cotton fibres.

▲ A textile factory in the 19th century was a grim place. The noise was deafening and accidents were common. Women and children worked long hours, six days a week, for low wages.

spinning frame

Using Metals

As the Industrial Revolution grew, iron and steel were needed more and more for machines and for the factories that made machines.

Iron-making

Long ago people made iron by putting the **ore** into a hot **charcoal** fire. They used bellows to force air into the fire to make it burn hotter. The melted iron collected in a lump. Abraham Darby discovered that **coke** made a hotter fire than charcoal. Air blown in by Watt's steam-engine produced a fire that was even hotter.

The secret of steel-making

Steel had been made for 4,000 years. But in 1722 René de Réaumur, a Frenchman, added carbon to steel to make it hard

▶ This steel-making furnace is loaded with scrap steel, iron ore, and limestone. Molten steel is then taken out.

hot gases

loading skip

firebrick lining

hot air

molten slag

molten iron

iron tap hole

◄ Iron is made in a blast-furnace like this. The furnace is lined with brick and cooled with water. Molten iron is taken out every few hours. Some furnaces can make 3,000 tonnes per day! Slag is the collection of all the impurities in iron ore.

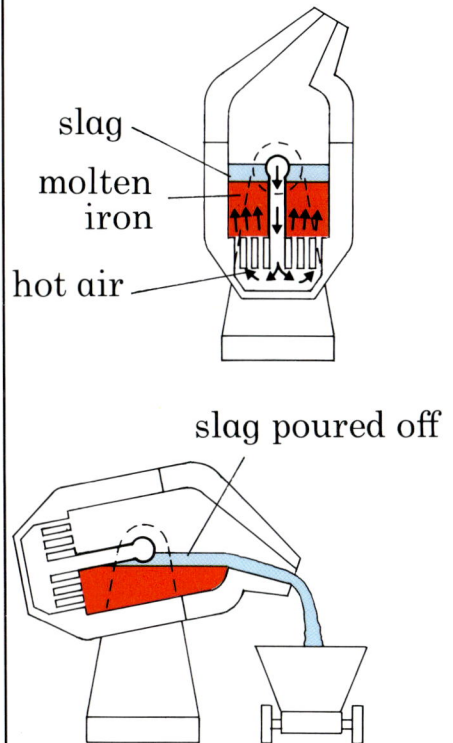

slag

molten iron

hot air

slag poured off

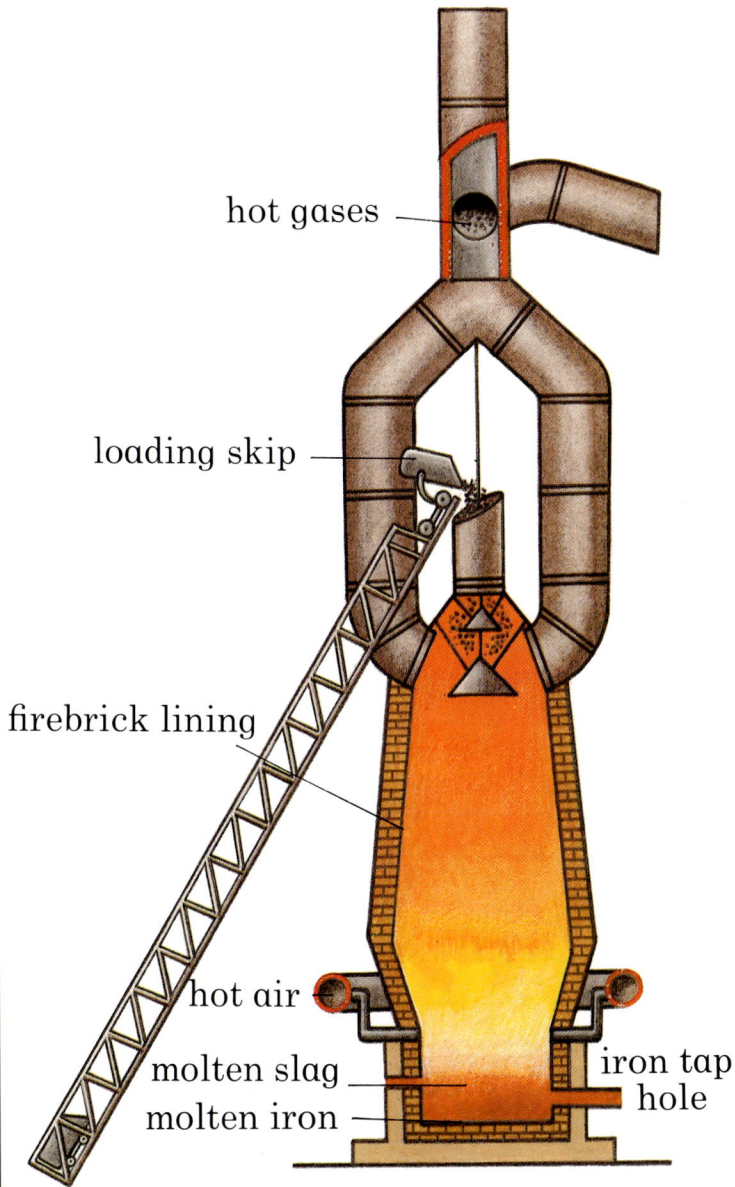

and springy for tools and machines. Gilchrist Thomas invented a steel furnace that was lined with limestone so it could use impure iron to make into steel. With this new furnace, steel production soared.

▲ Henry Bessemer invented the Bessemer converter for steel-making. It can tip to the side for adding limestone. Then it tips upright, and air blows into it from below to burn out the impurities from the iron.

Electricity Arrives

Static electricity

Comb your hair vigorously and the comb will pick up bits of fluff. This is static electricity at work. In 1745, a German clergyman named E. J. von Kleist invented the Leyden jar for storing static electricity. Touching the Leyden jar produced a spark.

Current electricity

When you turn on a light, current electricity lights up the bulb. It is like turning on a tap, but instead of water coming out, electricity

charged comb
paper

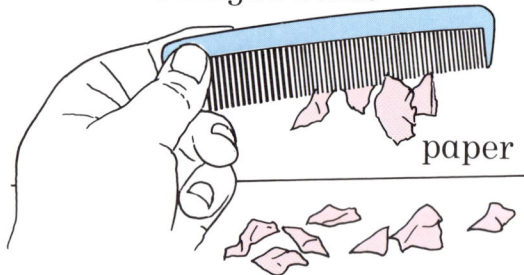

▲ Static electricity, made by rubbing a comb through your hair, can pick up small bits of paper with its positive charge.

▶ Volta's battery was made up of round discs of copper, zinc and cloth soaked in acid. With more discs added, Volta could make more powerful sparks.

◀ Michael Faraday invented the electric generator and the electric motor. Here he shows how magnets can make electricity.

sewing
thread
filament

flows. In 1800, Alessandro Volta invented an electric cell, or battery, that stored current electricity. In 1821 Michael Faraday discovered how to make current electricity by moving a magnet inside an electric coil. This led to large generators making electricity. By the 1890s, electricity lit up whole cities.

▲ Thomas Alva Edison, a great American inventor, made the first workable light bulb in 1879. He used a cotton thread in a glass bulb.

Farming and Food

Food facts

● In 1831, Cyrus Hall McCormick invented the reaper for cutting wheat.

● McCormick's factory in Chicago made 4,000 farm machines a year.

● Hippolyte Mégé Mouries of France invented margarine in 1870.

● In 1939, Franklin Kidd patented a fast method of freeze-drying food.

▶ This powerful modern tractor is pulling a disc plough. The cabin keeps the farmer from being crushed if the tractor tips over. This tractor has wheels, but others have caterpillar tracks.

Growing food

As more people moved to cities to find work and live, more cheap food was needed to feed them. Farmers began to grow food crops for sale. Several inventions helped to increase production. In England, farmers began using **drill ploughs** and horse **harrows**. In the United States, farmers used the newly-invented tractor and combine harvester.

Cooking and preserving

Denis Papin of France made the first pressure cooker that could

engine

pick-up reel

cutting bar

◄ The combine harvester is both a reaper and a thresher. It was widely used in the wheat plains of North America after 1917. Now, most farming countries use combine harvesters.

cans filled and sealed

steam heated to kill bacteria

cans ready for labelling

◄ Canning is one way of preserving food so it will not spoil. Fruit, meat and vegetables are canned in very clean factories. Food will stay fresh for a year or more in cans. Englishman Peter Durand first put food in cans in the 1800s.

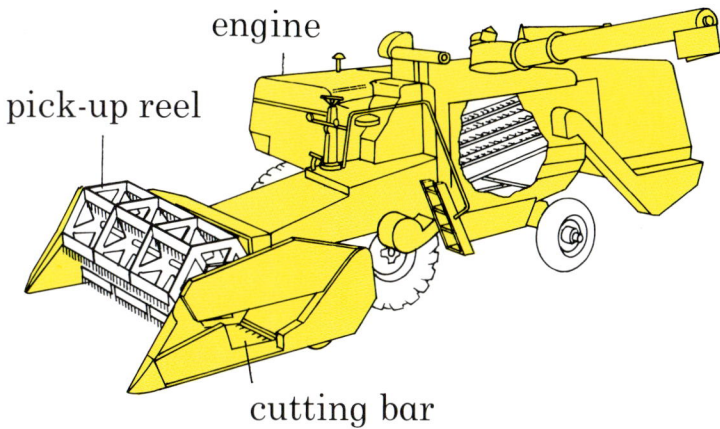

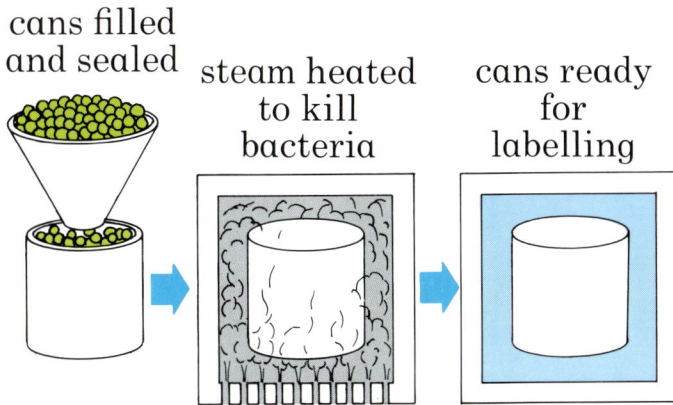

cook foods hotter and faster. Nicolas Appert invented the process of bottling fruit. Later metal cans were used. The quick-freezing of foods came in the 1920s. Today we add chemicals to some foods to keep them from spoiling.

Around 1770, Joseph Priestley added carbon dioxide gas to water, hoping it would cure the disease scurvy. It didn't. But it made a pleasant drink, soda water.

▲ Joseph Priestley (1733-1804) was a British chemist.

Oil and Gas

▶ Opposite right: this drilling platform in the North Sea drills into the seabed to reach the gas underneath the rock.

Oil facts

● Abraham Gesner, of Canada, learned how to get paraffin from crude oil by heating it.

● In 1859, Edwin Drake struck oil in Pennsylvania, USA.

▶ Gasoline, diesel oil and other products come from oil refineries like the one shown here.

The oil industry

People have used petroleum since ancient times. In the Bible Noah waterproofed his ark with pitch, a kind of petroleum. The Egyptians used petroleum to grease chariot axles. Inventions for getting **paraffin** from oil came in the 1850s. Paraffin was burned in lamps and stoves. Edwin L. Drake started the oil industry when he drilled the first deep oil well in 1859. Samuel van Syckel built the first oil pipeline. Today, pipes carry oil for thousands of miles.

warm cabinet

hook for hanging meat

gas flame

▲ Homes in the 1800s used gas ovens like this one.

The gas industry

In 1792, William Murdock invented gas lighting to replace candles. By 1850 many towns in Europe and North America were using gas to light their streets and houses. In 1832 James Sharp invented gas stoves for cooking. Soon these were in use throughout the United States and Britain. Most gas used in Britain today is natural gas, from wells in the North Sea. The United States also has natural gas wells.

Gas facts

● In 1780 Frenchman Antoine Lavoisier invented a gas-holding storage tank.

● Frederick Albert Winsor, of Germany, formed the world's first gas company in 1813.

● Robert Bunsen developed the gas Bunsen burner that is widely used in laboratories. It gives a steady heat by mixing air with the gas through a hole at the bottom of the burner.

CHAPTER SEVEN

INVENTIONS TODAY

Mass Production

Over the years the demand for all sorts of goods has greatly increased. To meet these demands, factories had to find quicker and cheaper ways of making their goods. In America, Eli Whitney set up a gun factory in 1798 that made exactly similar parts. These parts could be put together in the same way. This was the start of mass production.

▼ These cars are rolling off the final assembly line at the Ford Motor Company in Detroit, USA. The car body slid down a ramp and landed on its wheels.

CUGNOT'S TRACTION ENGINE.

The motor car

In 1769, Nicolas Cugnot made the first successful steam-driven car. In the late 1800s, electric cars became popular after Camille Faure invented a car battery to store electricity. The first car to run on gas was built by Etienne Lenoir in 1860. Ransom E. Olds built cars by using an **assembly line**, but it was Henry Ford who perfected this method of manufacturing. Ford built his famous Model T Ford, which was very cheap for its day. In this way the modern car industry began. Today, car factories use computer-controlled robots to do the work that humans once did.

▲ Nicolas Cugnot's steam traction engine, built in the 1760s, was the first true motor car. It had a single front wheel. In front of it hung the boiler and engine.

▲ Karl Benz, who built the first petrol-driven car for sale to the public.

Flight

Montgolfier brothers' balloon

▶ Here are three kinds of flying machines: a hot-air balloon (left), a biplane (middle), and an airship (right). The balloon was flown in front of King Louis XVI of France. Early biplanes had fixed wheels for landing. *La France* could travel at the speed of 14 mph!

People have always dreamed of flying. The first flight was made by the Montgolfier brothers in a balloon in 1783. In 1804, Sir George Cayley invented a glider. Arthur Renard and Charles Krebs made *La France*, the first steam-powered airship, in 1884. The Wright brothers built the first powered aeroplane in 1903. They had to invent all the parts themselves, including the engine. Early planes were biplanes, with two sets of wings. They were made of fabric and wood. In the 1920s, the first metal aeroplanes were made.

a biplane

La France

The jet and space age

Jet-engine aeroplanes can fly faster than propeller planes – some even faster than the speed of sound! Pilot Chuck Yeager first broke the sound barrier in 1947. The Soviet Union launched the first person into space, Major Yuri Gagarin, in 1961. In 1969, Neil Armstrong was the first person to walk on the Moon. Soviet and the US space programmers hope to land a person on Mars.

▲ A space shuttle is launched from the Kennedy Space Center in Florida, USA.

◀ Chuck Yeager broke the sound barrier in 1947 with his Bell X-1 plane.

Sending Messages

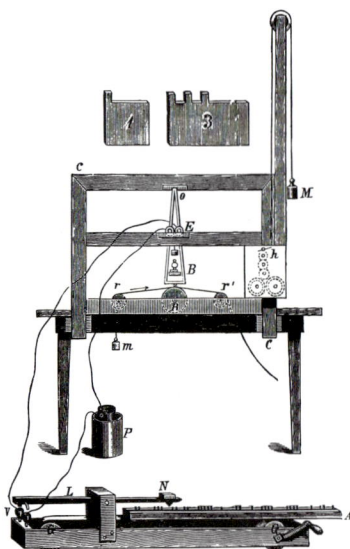

Modern **communication** began in 1844 when Samuel Morse invented the telegraph. In 1876 Alexander Graham Bell invented the telephone. By the 1920s, radio, invented by Guglielmo Marconi, was popular in homes.

Photography and cinema

The first photograph was taken by Joseph Nicéphore Niepce in 1826. Cameras evolved during the next century until, by 1947, a Polaroid Land camera could take pictures that developed in only 60 seconds. Moving films were first made in the 1890s. In 1927, sound was successfully added.

Television

Two inventions made television possible: the photo-electric cell

▲ Here is a sketch of Samuel Morse's first electric telegraph. It sent out messages in a series of dots and dashes, called Morse code.

▶ This picture was taken by the space shuttle *Discovery*. It shows a communications satellite going round Earth.

aerial

electron beams

decoders

electron guns

beam deflectors

screen

shadow mask

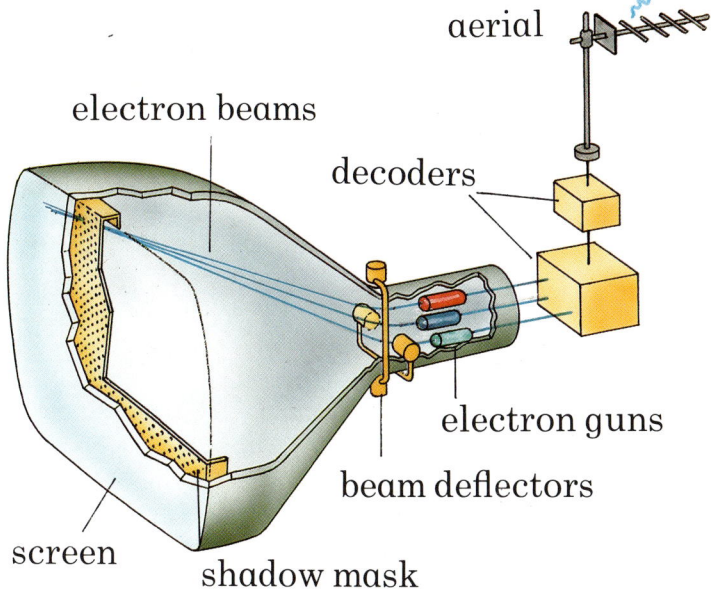

◄ The television aerial
picks up signals from the
television station. These
are shot onto the screen.
The shadow mask guides
the beams to strike dots on
the screen that are
coloured either red, green,
or blue.

that turned light into electric
current and the Crookes tube
that changed the electric current
back into light. After World War
II, TV became very popular.
Colour TV began in the United
States in 1953. In 1962, the first
TV message went via **satellite**. In
1965 a US space probe sent TV
pictures of Mars to Earth.

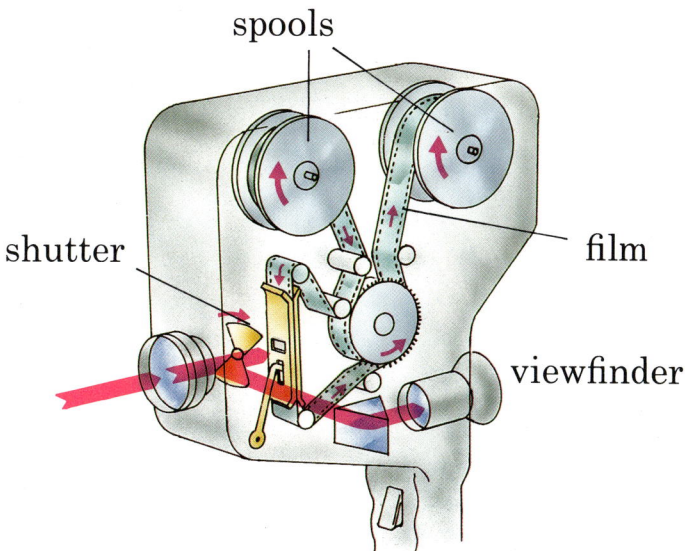

Communication facts

● The first words Bell
spoke into his telephone
were 'Mr. Watson, come
here! I want you!'

● The first words Thomas
Edison recorded on his
phonograph, or talking
machine, were 'Mary had
a little lamb'.

● Baron Jons Berzelius
invented the photo-cell
that turned light signals
into electric current.

● Three main inventors of
television were Philo T.
Farnsworth, John Logie
Baird and Vladimir
Zworykin.

spools

film

shutter

viewfinder

◄ A movie camera takes
pictures the same way a
still camera does. The film
is divided into frames
and the camera stops for a
split-second for each
frame to be shot.

The Computer and the Future

▶ A sketch of Charles Babbage's design for a calculator, a type of computer. As the user fed in numbers, cogs turned to give the answer.

▲ New computers are designed and tested in laboratories like this.

When Charles Babbage began working on his calculating machine in 1832, he little dreamt what it would lead to. His invention was the first that resembled our modern-day computer. However, it was never completed. Over a century later, in 1945, the first electronic computer was built in the United States. Computers now control airport traffic, road traffic, nuclear power stations, car factories and coal-mines. They can even translate from one language to another.

Tomorrow's inventor

It isn't likely that a person without a science background will invent things in the future. The days of the amateur inventor, such as Thomas Edison, are coming to an end. Edison's work in electricity, telegraphy, moving pictures and sound recording paved new ways for science and industry to follow. Today, people working as teams in well-equipped laboratories invent most of our new gadgets and machines. Perhaps computers will be the inventors of tomorrow.

▲ An artist's idea of what a space station in the future may look like.

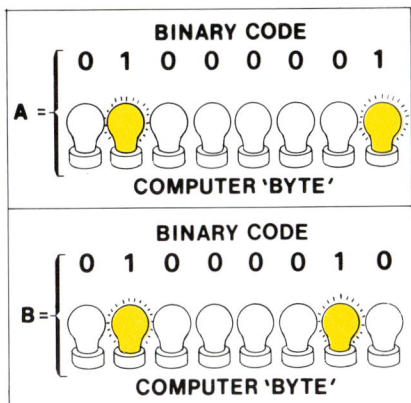

BINARY CODE

A = 0 1 0 0 0 0 0 1

COMPUTER 'BYTE'

BINARY CODE

B = 0 1 0 0 0 0 1 0

COMPUTER 'BYTE'

▲ Computers work with on/off switches that represent binary numbers, made up of only 1s and 0s. Shown here are the numbers 65 and 66.

Glossary

Assembly line: in an assembly line every worker does a different job at a different stage on the same product.

Axle: a pin or rod attached to the centre of a wheel. At the other end of the rod is another wheel attached in the same way. This rod is the axle. It stays still while the wheels turn.

Bacteria: these are very, very small living things that can only be seen under a microscope. Some bacteria can make you ill.

Ballistics: the study of the movement in air of objects that have been thrown or shot, such as an arrow, cannon ball or bullet.

Bamboo: a huge grass that grows wild in very hot countries. It is hollow and looks like wood.

Cretans: these are people who live on the island of Crete in the Mediterranean Sea. This island is now part of Greece.

Charcoal: when wood is burned in little air, it turns into charcoal.

Coke: coal that has been heated and made purer. It used as fuel.

Communication: passing information amongst people or groups of people. Talking or writing are both ways of communicating.

Condense: this is the action of reducing something to a thicker and heavier form. For example, steam condenses when it cools down to form water.

Crank: an arm which links and drives moving parts in a machine.

Cylinder: this is a word used to describe a sealed round tube.

Drill plough: this is a machine that makes holes in the earth into which grain is dropped and left to grow.

Fabric: cloth that has been made in a factory.

Galley: a long ship with one deck that moves through the water using oars and a sail.

Gears: a system of cogs (toothed wheels) that transfers movement from one part of a machine to another part.

Harness: the leather gear put on horses or oxen to lead and control them. It has parts like the bridle and reins.

Harrow: a machine used by a farmer to break up the earth into smaller pieces before planting seeds.

Industrial Revolution: a period from about 1750 to 1850 when the use of machines and the growth of factories spread quickly.

Keel: a flat piece of wood or metal fixed to the bottom of a boat; it extends downwards in the water. It stops the boat from tipping over.

Magnetic: this word describes an object that is able to attract other objects, usually made from metals like iron and steel.

Magnify: to make an object look larger and clearer using lenses. People with short sight wear glasses to magnify things.

Mechanical: this word describes anything to do with tools or implements made by people to help in improving their lives.

Meteorites: chunks of stone or metal that strike Earth from outer space.

Navigation: the science of finding the way from one place to another.

Ore: a natural substance found in the Earth that contains pieces of pure metal. For example, iron comes from iron ore.

Paraffin: a liquid made from carbon and hydrogen and which comes from petroleum.

Patents: these are given out by law to anyone who has thought of an invention and proved that it is their invention. It gives them the right to make, use and sell their invention or to let other people make, use and sell it.

Pulley: wheels over which ropes or chains run. They lift things up more better.

Radio waves: these are signals that can be sent through space without the use of wires. They can be picked up by radios. This is why the first radio was called a 'wireless'.

Renaissance: a time in history between about 1420 and 1520 when people became interested in the art and science of ancient Greece and Rome. It inspired them in their own artistic and scientific efforts.

Satellite: something that goes round a planet, like the Earth's Moon. Man-made satellites are launched from Earth.

Semites: a group of people who spoke Semitic, an early Middle East language. They include Assyrians, Hebrews, Carthaginians and Phoenicians.

Smelt: this word means to melt ore using a hot oven or furnace in order to separate the metal it contains from other substances in the ore.

Stern-post rudder: a flat piece of wood or metal that sticks out from the back of a boat (the stern); it is used for steering.

Stirrups: iron loops with a flattened base hanging by a strap from a saddle for the rider to put his or her feet in.

Sumerians: people who lived in Sumer, Mesopotamia, a land between the rivers Tigris and Euphrates, around 3,000 BC.

Thermometer: this is a device that measures how hot or how cold something is.

Token: a sign, symbol or mark. Token money was once used. The coin had no value in itself, only what it stood for.

Trip hammer: a high-speed, power-driven hammer used to shape tools or machine parts.

Vacuum: this is a word to describe an empty space, which has no air in it.

Vaulting: this word describes a roof or ceiling that is arched or curved. Lots of cathedrals have vaulted ceilings.

Yarn: pieces of either wool, silk, cotton or flax that are spun for use in weaving or knitting.

Yoke: a curved piece of wood placed over horses' or oxen's necks and fastened to a plough or cart that the animals pull along.

Zero: this is a word used to describe nought. It is a number which has no value. Imagine if we did not have zero, how would we be able to write 100?

Index

A number in **bold** shows the entry is illustrated on that page. The same page often has writing about the entry too.